Community Helpers

Child Care Providers

by Erika S. Manley

Bullfrog Books

Ideas for Parents and Teachers

Bullfrog Books let children practice reading informational text at the earliest reading levels. Repetition, familiar words, and photo labels support early readers.

Before Reading
- Discuss the cover photo. What does it tell them?

- Look at the picture glossary together. Read and discuss the words.

Read the Book
- "Walk" through the book and look at the photos. Let the child ask questions. Point out the photo labels.

- Read the book to the child, or have him or her read independently.

After Reading
- Prompt the child to think more. Ask: Have you ever had a babysitter? Have you spent time at a daycare? What sorts of things did you do?

Bullfrog Books are published by Jump!
5357 Penn Avenue South
Minneapolis, MN 55419
www.jumplibrary.com

Library of Congress Cataloging-in-Publication Data

Names: Manley, Erika S., author.
Title: Child care providers / by Erika S. Manley.
Description: Minneapolis, Minnesota: Jump!, Inc., [2017] | Series: Community helpers | Includes index.
Audience: Age: 5–8. | Audience: K to Grade 3.
Identifiers: LCCN 2016047272 (print)
LCCN 2016049481 (ebook)
ISBN 9781620316726 (hardcover: alk. paper)
ISBN 9781620317259 (pbk.)
ISBN 9781624965494 (ebook)
Subjects: LCSH: Child care—Juvenile literature.
Communities—Juvenile literature.
Classification: LCC HQ778.5 .M36 2017 (print)
LCC HQ778.5 (ebook) | DDC 362.7—dc23
LC record available at https://lccn.loc.gov/2016047272

Editor: Jenny Fretland VanVoorst
Book Designer: Leah Sanders
Photo Researcher: Leah Sanders

Photo Credits: Africa Studio/Shutterstock, cover; pikselstock/Shutterstock, cover; lenetstan/Shutterstock, 1; Antonova Anna/Shutterstock, 3; khoa vu/Getty, 4; Image Source/Getty, 5; Lordn/iStock, 6–7; Weekend Images Inc./Getty, 8, 10–11; Hill Street Studios/Getty, 9; eurobanks/Shutterstock, 12–13; wavebreakmedia/Shutterstock, 12–13; RuslanDashinsky/Getty, 14–15; DGLimages/Shutterstock, 16, 17; FatCamera/iStock, 18–19; svetikd/Getty, 20–21; Beloborod/Shutterstock, 22; Billion Photos/Shutterstock, 24.

Printed in the United States of America at Corporate Graphics in North Mankato, Minnesota.

Table of Contents

Play and Learn 4

At the Daycare 22

Picture Glossary 23

Index 24

To Learn More 24

Play and Learn

Ellie wants to be a child care provider.

What do they do?

They take care of us.

They play with us.

They help us learn.

Ms. Kim cares for kids in her home.

She watches them play outside.

She makes sure they are safe.

9

Ms. Kim reads a story.

Everyone listens.

Wow! The story
is exciting!

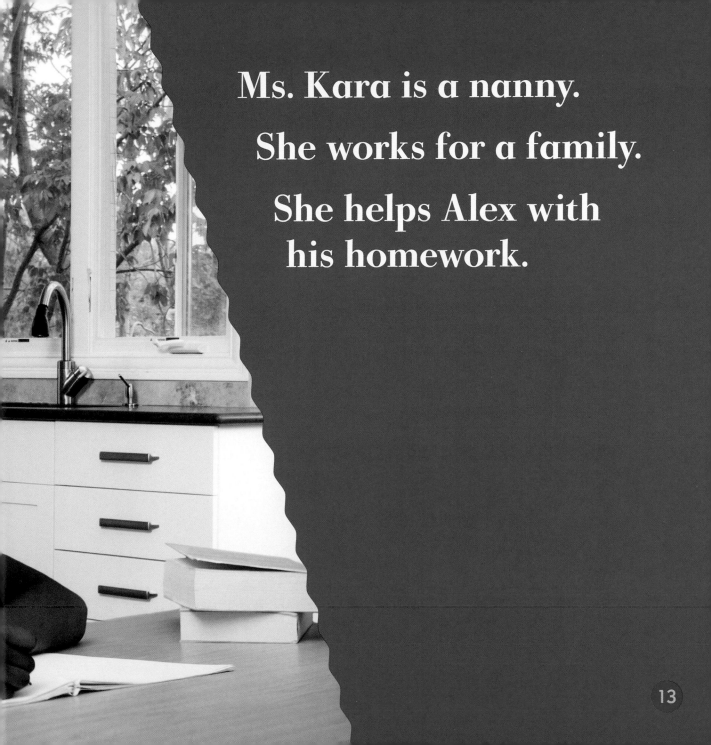

Ms. Kara is a nanny.

She works for a family.

She helps Alex with
his homework.

She changes
Kit's diaper.

Phew!

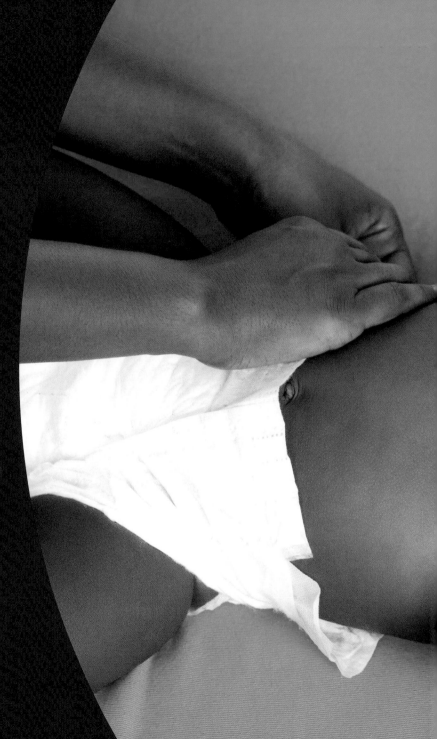

Mr. Vic works at a daycare center.

water
table

He sets up a water table.

Kids can play and learn.

Splash!

Snack time!

Mr. Vic passes out
fruit and milk.

Ali has an apple.

So does Kate.

Yum!

Child care providers
do good work!

At the Daycare

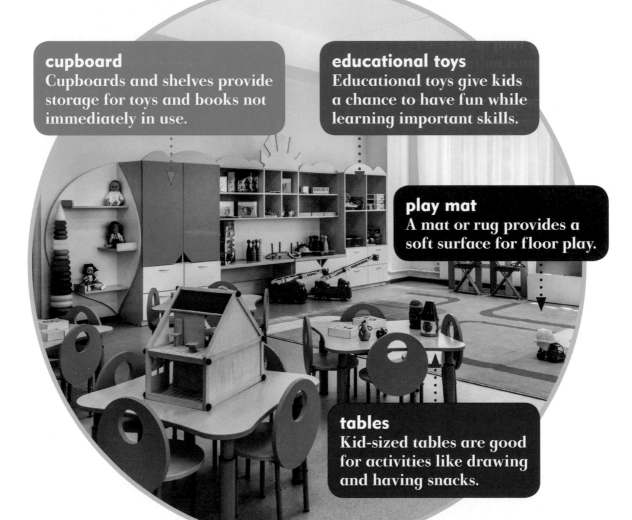

cupboard
Cupboards and shelves provide storage for toys and books not immediately in use.

educational toys
Educational toys give kids a chance to have fun while learning important skills.

play mat
A mat or rug provides a soft surface for floor play.

tables
Kid-sized tables are good for activities like drawing and having snacks.

Picture Glossary

daycare
A place where children are cared for during the day.

nanny
A person employed to care for children in a household.

homework
Assignments that are to be completed outside of school.

provider
A person who does a job or offers a service.

Index

daycare 16

diaper 14

home 8

homework 13

learn 7, 17

nanny 13

outside 9

play 7, 9, 17

safe 9

snack 19

story 10

water table 17

To Learn More

Learning more is as easy as 1, 2, 3.

1) Go to www.factsurfer.com

2) Enter "childcareproviders" into the search box.

3) Click the "Surf" button to see a list of websites.

With factsurfer.com, finding more information is just a click away.